Weep No More
God Has Not Forgotten You!

by

Olu Sobanjo

Regina Kehinde

& Other Amazing Contributors

WEEP NO MORE
God Has Not Forgotten You

ISBN – 978-0-9781595-7-3

Published by Grace Press
Kingston, Ontario, Canada.

www.GracePress.com

Dedication

To my darling Mom, Grace Tinuola Olowosoyo, a strong and exceptionally loving woman, who agreed to the path of life that brought me here, and went through thick and thins for her children. I am lost for words to describe what having you as my Mom has been to me.

I am so grateful for your support and advice that are always founded on the truth of the word of God, and for your godly example as a wife, mom, and servant of the Most High.

I am indeed blessed to call you my mentor in life and ministry. I thank God for you and pray that you will continue to flourish in Christ, and He will continually be formed in you.

Love You Mom!

Acknowledgements

*I've enjoyed the help and support of many people,
far and near. I want to say thank you all.*

To you my darling friend, pastor and lover, Ade So-banjo — It's a blessing to live life in partnership with you. Thanks for allowing me time to do all that God has called me to do and for writing the foreword for this book. All those stunts that we do and all our discoveries together make life a lot more meaningful. You my darling continue to convince me that there is indeed a heaven, and one doesn't need to die to get there. Love you.

To my two wonderful sons, Demi and Damilola — Thanks for your understanding while I needed some silence around the house. It's great to see you read the book while I took a break from writing. It's amazing that both of you are now able to make major contributions to the work we do as a family including this book, thanks boys!

To Rev. Mrs. Regina Kehinde — Thanks for agreeing to work superfast on the book as to the edits and re-writes where necessary; and for all your gifts always and labour of love.

To my dear sister-in-law, Dr. Bola — Thanks for your friendship and for always being available to edit my work.

To everyone that God has added to my life through Overcomers Assembly and Overcomers Fellowship International — I am so grateful that God continues to teach me to know Him more through you all. I have been blessed with amazing friends, sisters, brothers, daughters and grandkids in you all. And I pray for you always that you will all continue to shine brightly for the Lord.

To all the amazing people that contributed their tes-timonies towards this work — Thanks for pouring out of you so that others may be enriched. To my elder brother, Pastor Kunle Olowosoyo, and to Pastor Cary Lee Carter, Dr. Mrs. Helen Njoku, Pastor Jean Yves Ntone, Grandma Fern Bath, Pastor Tope Taiwo, Olu-watobiloba Moody, Rotimi Odekeye, my namesake and friend Oluwaseun Adesina, and others who chose to write as anonymous. Thanks!

And to my parents and parents-in-law — Thanks for your support and love always. I am so grateful to have you both in my life.

To everyone that has given me the opportunity of personally mentoring them, thank you. I am eternally grateful to God for you. And I want to continue to learn through you.

Finally, to all my friends and family members all over the world. Thanks. I pray that you will live daily knowing that God cares about you. God bless you all.

Foreword

Everybody needs an encouragement from time to time! In the early days of my walk with Christ, I loved reading books, which had lots of testimonies, so I went hunting for biographies and autobiography. What was I looking for? I wanted proof that a person living in the world at that time (not a biblical character) could practice these truths that I was reading about in Scriptures. Over the years, I have found many examples, and it still gives me great joy when the life of a person is proof that God is real today.

In "Weep Not! God has not forgotten you," you will find many stories (testimonies) that will make your heart glad about the reality of God. These testimonies address various challenges that we all face in life. Not only will the testimonies encourage you as a believer, there are nuggets of truth that will seep into your spirit.

After reading this book, I could not but appreciate the faithfulness of our Lord Jesus Christ.

Pastor Olu is my best friend and companion. I have seen her grow in her walk with God over the last 15 years. She loves to see believers get real with God and enjoy their relationship with our Lord Jesus. In this book, she takes this love to a new level by inviting other believers (many people that I know and respect) to be part of this beautiful project of encouraging others in their walk with God.

This is another work that will encourage you to trust God and live the life of God from the inside out! I believe this book will encourage you, too!

Ade Sobanjo

Table of Content

Introduction

One moment, you are having a peaceful day, enjoying every second, sipping your favorite cup of tea (or juice), with no stress, pain, or panic. And your loved ones are doing well on the other side of town; your projects are progressing beautifully—you feel like you are on top of the world. Then all of a sudden, a storm arises and everything seems to change. Calm turns to chaos and peace to panic. Suddenly, you begin to wonder if God has gone on vacation in a no-network zone where He couldn't be reached.

It's hard even for most believers to remain calm and remember that God has not forgotten them when they seem to be on the raging sea of life, being tossed mercilessly. Can you relate to that scenario? You are discouraged, thinking all is lost, and heavily burdened with a load of care, as the cross you are called to carry seems too heavy to bear. Comparing your experience with others', you feel like it's a visit to hell while it's heaven for them.

If you have ever been in a storm, I am sure you know what I mean. Or maybe you are actually in the middle of one right now. Funny enough, though the name of the storm might sound Christianly like Katrina, but it doesn't have anything like Christ in what it brings—a storm is a storm, nothing more. If this is you, you have the right book you need today. If, on the other hand, you don't have any storms raging right now, praise God! I want you to read on though, for you will learn a thing or two in preparation for what may be ahead of you.

The book you are holding is one that God laid on my heart to write on a day I was beautifully blessed by the ministry of a wonderful woman of God, Rev. Mrs. Regina Kehinde. She was a guest at our home for the very first time since I met her through my darling husband around 1999.

My family and I had moved from Canada to Nigeria to plant a new branch of Overcomers. We had been there for about a year when she came visiting. While living in Canada, we visited her in her New York home a couple of times but we were never privileged to have her visit us due to her busy schedules and others variables. As soon as we knew she was coming to Nigeria, we started to plan to have her stay over with us, and minister to the members of our new church family in Kuje.

Thankfully, God made it possible. It was a special time of fellowship at home. There was a lot of catching ups to do. At church, I was off kid's church duty on this particular day so I could enjoy her ministry at the church service.

An amazing thing happened to me on this particular day. I was so overwhelmed and excited in my spirit as soon as she announced the title of her sermon: Weep No More, You Are Not Forgotten. My spirit was lifted, and my heart began to skip for joy. My zeal level went up. And the rest of the time was extremely refreshing. I suddenly had the zeal that I did not realize was even lost. The bizarre thing is that I didn't even think I was weeping. However, when the message came, I was so excited to know that I had not been forgotten.

Funny as it may seem, I had been missing my Canadian comfort, the people, the system, and the life. I felt the sacrifice required of me to do God's will didn't mean anything to God. What is my comfort compared to the millions of Christian lives that have been sacrificed for the kingdom? Souls are perishing; the harvest is plenty, and there is no room for comfort. Even though I seemed to be OK with my new world, I was seriously missing the life I had lived in the past 10 years. However, at that moment, God Himself began to whisper into my ears as a loving father would: How could you ever think I forgot you? How could you imagine that your labour is insignificant? I thought you and I were just talking the other day about how much I love the time we spend together. How excited and pleasurable you make me feel when you pour out praises from your heart to me.

As she continued with her sermon, I heard those sweet words from my heavenly Father. Oh, how comforted my spirit became after that! That moment, I got a fresh reminder of how important the work I was doing was in God's perspective. And that was the moment I got a desire to work on this book. I wanted to bring the same message to you so that your joy may be full. I couldn't wait till the end of the service to announce to my hubby and Mummy Kehinde that her sermon would birth a book that will be given to each lady at our 10th annual ladies' conference (Vessels of Grace Conference) in May of 2016.

As I prayed further about this project, I heard God say to ask some other wonderful believers around the world to contribute towards the work; and I am happy to say that you are holding a book of hope. My prayer is that as you read this book, you will find a verse of the scripture, a testimony, or revelations that will bring you hope in Jesus' name. I pray that you will fully know that God is always with you as He promised.

That special sermon, which stirred my spirit on that day, has been converted into the next section in this book, followed by series of wonderful testimonies that will help you turn your heart to God, even in the middle of your many trials. The final section is rich in treasure and promises that will help you to put your trust in the Lord. I am sure; the whole book will bless you. Christ was actually asleep on the boat amidst a storm, but He has power and authority to calm any storm only if we call on Him and only Him.

1

You Are Not Forgotten

By Rev. Mrs. Regina Kehinde

Exodus 3:1- 22

Moses' father-in-law was named Jethro. Jethro was a priest of Midian. Moses took care of Jethro's sheep. One day Moses led the sheep to the west side of the desert. He went to a mountain called Horeb, the mountain of God. 2 On that mountain, Moses saw the angel of the LORD in a burning bush.

Moses saw a bush that was burning without being destroyed. 3 So he decided to go closer to the bush and see how a bush could continue burning without being burned up.

4 The LORD saw Moses was coming to look at the bush. So he called to him from the bush. He said, "Moses, Moses!"

Moses said, "Yes, Lord."

5 Then God said, "Don't come any closer. Take off your sandals. You are standing on holy ground. 6 I am the God of your ancestors. I am the God of Abraham, the God of Isaac, and the God of Jacob."

Moses covered his face because he was afraid to look at God.

7 Then the LORD said, "I have seen the troubles my people have suffered in Egypt, and I have heard their cries when the Egyptians hurt them. I know about their pain. 8 Now I will go down and save my people from the Egyptians. I will take them from that land and lead them to a good land where they can be free from these troubles. It is a land filled with many good things. Many different people live in that land: the Canaanites, Hittites, Amorites, Perizzites, Hivites, and Jebusites. 9 I have heard the cries of the Israelites, and I have seen the way the Egyptians have made life hard for them. 10 So now I am sending you to Pharaoh. Go! Lead my people, the Israelites, out of Egypt."

The children of Israel were in the land of Egypt for four hundred and thirty (430) years, working like elephants but eating like ants. Although they might not be sick, having the Great Physician as their God, they were still in slavery and bondage. The gruesome fatigue at bedtime and the fear of the slave work at dawn must have brought them sorrow every day. As they go to work in the morning, I can hear each of them saying, "The toil and slavery continues."

The agony was so much on their hearts that, as the Bible reveals in the text above, God saw their sorrows, He saw their pains, and He heard their cries; so, in response to their agony, God said it was time to deliver them. I don't know who is reading this right now; God is giving you His word of reassurance, saying, "You're not forgotten." No matter how long you've toiled and laboured and even if it seems as if your efforts have no obvious reward, you are not forgotten. "The deal is still on," quoting the words of Foursquare President, Pastor Jack Hayford.

God is the God that makes the deal and the deal is still on. You have never been forgotten and you will never be forgotten. Regardless of what you're going through, maybe you are working for people or for yourself and you have nothing to show for it, you are not forgotten. Your day of rewards is here. God says you should remember His words—you're not forgotten; therefore, weep no more.

WHY TEARS

Weeping endures for so many reasons, whether night or day. Here are a few reasons:

- The pain a wayward child brings to a parent

- The pain of bareness or miscarriages in a home

- The pain of sickness

- The pain of poverty

There are so many reasons why people weep. Many a times you don't even want people to see that you are weeping—suffering from a specific storm of life—but you are. If this is you dearly beloved, weep no more!

Thank God for the Psalmist that says, ''*Weeping may endure for a night but there's joy coming in the morning*'' (Psalm 30: 5).

I thank God that today is your morning. Regardless of whatever has made you downcast, discouraged, or demobilised, and even if you think the end has come for you, you have not been forgotten. God says that the deal is still on. Weep no more.

EXAMPLES OF THOSE THAT RECEIVED God's WEEP-NO-MORE Charge

The Bible is filled with numerous examples of those who received the "weep no more" intervention of God—a kind of reassurance from God that all would be well. Like most people in distress, they felt the agony of the storm and must have felt as if they had been forgotten, but God came to their rescue saying, "The deal is still on," because He did not forget or forsake them. The following are a few:

The Israelites

As earlier mentioned, when the Israelites were in slavery, hardship, and pains, it was not palatable. For over 400 years—that means more than 4 generations—they were having children, they were getting married but they were slaves and in terrible bondage.

In February of 1994, I had the opportunity to visit Egypt. I went out by myself leaving my husband in the hotel; I couldn't wait to see the land of Goshen. I wanted to see where the Israelites lived in Egypt in the days of slavery. I wanted to have an idea of what they were delivered from. I noticed two things the moment I crossed the Nile Bridge from Cairo and got to the land of Goshen:

1. The houses in Goshen were never the same as in Cairo. The ones in Goshen were dilapidated, and they were mud houses. But in Cairo, you have gorgeous buildings—tall and magnificent to behold.

2. And then, I could see the peace and tranquility in Goshen.

The place was peaceful and wonderful, and the people's faces were very beautiful and calm. What a difference! Even many years after that Exodus of Israelites, as I noticed, there was peace in the lives of those living in Goshen.

It means the Israelites had peace even when they were in calamity and slavery; that peace will attend to you today in Jesus' name. I saw peace, and everything was just peaceful. When God says, "You are not forgotten," He means it. He told Israel, saying, "I have come to deliver you," and they were delivered. God said to Moses, "I have come to take them out of slavery, I have come to take them out of bondage, and I have come to take them out of the pain they are going through, because I have not forgotten them." God has not forgotten you. Do you believe it?

Mephibosheth

The second example we want to see is the man that is called Mephibosheth in 2 Samuel Chapter 9. The Bible tells us that there was war, and everybody was running for his or her lives; and Saul's family was destroyed except a little baby called Mephibosheth. Ziba was a servant of Saul and nanny to this baby. Ziba tried to safe Mephibosheth during the war, and as he was running with the baby in his arms, he stumbled, and Mephibosheth fell and became paralyzed on the two legs.

Instead of taking care of the child, Ziba took over all the property and assets that Saul had including that of Saul's only surviving grandson. He put Mephibosheth in an unsecured and obscured place called Lo-debar where Mephibosheth grew up. He was thrown out of his inheritance, and lived like a beggar in the hands of Ziba, his grandfather's servant. On a particular day, David just rose and said, "Is there yet anyone in the household of Saul so that I may do him good for the sake of Jonathan my friend?" I pray that somebody will do you good for the sake of Jesus, and for the sake of Calvary, somebody will rise up and come to you, saying, "Well, this is what you've done in the time past, and I want to do you good now because of Jesus whom you serve." They may even say that their kind gesture is because of your father or mother—something must cause something.

I decree that your blessings, your favor, your merit, your prosperity that is being withheld in the hands of some-body shall be released to you in the Name of Jesus. Today, by the grace of God and by the authority I have in Christ, if you were in obscurity before now and nobody knew you, you worked like an elephant but you ate like an ant, and you are kept in Lo-debar, I say today, just as David called for Mephibosheth, you will be called out in Jesus name. Your boss will call you out, your master will call you out, and your partners in business will call you out. You will come out of obscurity, you will be in the limelight, and you will begin to live the life of prosperity with God! So shall it be in Jesus' Name.

David said, "Is there anyone left in the house of Saul that I may do kindness unto him for the sake of my friend Jonathan," and they mentioned to him that Mephibosheth was the only survivor of Saul's household. He asked them to call Ziba, the servant in the household of Saul. And when he came he said, "Eh! There is nobody, except a lame man...well, he is of no use." Can you imagine the humiliation? How can somebody say you are of no use, when God has not given up on you? Since God has saved your soul, you will be of use to everybody around you, to your nation, to your city, to your job, in the Name of Jesus!

When my biological father passed on in 1977, though I am not the first-born, they couldn't make any decision until they found me. Can you imagine that? In your job, in your offices, they will not make positive decision until they find you, in the Name of Jesus. You will have a voice to the glory of His Name. So, Mephibosheth was brought to the King, even in his fear, hoping that he wasn't in any trouble with the king. The king said, "Don't worry, you will eat with me continually, and a particular ration will be given to you and you will be satisfied." He lived for the rest of his lifetime that kind of poor life. That is the life you shall live in Jesus' name—a life of no lack, a life of surplus and plenty.

Though you may not be physically lame or paralyzed, I declare that every form of paralysis in your life be terminated today, and you will live a life that glows in prosperity, in the Name of Jesus.

Let's take two more examples.

Jehoiakim

King Jehoiakim of Judah, in 2 Kings 25:27-30, was a captive taken to another strange land, and after having been dressed with the prison garments, he was put into prison. May the Lord release you from the prison of life, and your incarceration is over in Jesus' name. And the Bible says that there was a king called Evil-Merodak—what a name—who gave an order that Jehoiakim be brought out of the prison. And Jehoiakim was brought to the king, and his story changed completely, for his prison cloths were taken off and he had a daily ration allotted to him every day.

I decree to you and for you that every clothing that you have been known with, it may be in form of your shame or a label that makes people speak against you is torn apart and destroyed in the Name of Jesus. Every evil mark that the enemy has put on you in form of an image that you carry about, which blocks your progress, is removed from your life in the name of Jesus. In the Name of Jesus, may the anointing of God release you from incarceration now!

The Canaanite Woman

Our final example will be the Canaanite woman whose daughter was possessed with an evil spirit (Matthew 15:22-28). The woman came to Jesus Christ and said, "Master, my daughter is demon possessed," but Jesus completely ignored her. Even the disciples were sick and tired of her and her trouble, they begged Jesus to send her away; Jesus still did not respond. After a while, Jesus responded by telling her that He came for the Jews, and that it wasn't good to give the children's bread to dogs. Her response to Jesus was in agreement with His, and that the dogs could eat from the crumbs falling from the table.

That was faith. Jesus then said, "I have never seen this type of faith, not even in Israel." And instantly, her daughter was made whole.

Do you have a heartache in your family? Is your child, spouse, parents, or whoever is within the confines of your family relationship passing through pains? Because God and Jesus is the Great Physician, may the healing power of God come upon that person, and peace upon you, in Jesus' Name.

Praise the Lord!

Weep no more. You are not forgotten.

A present-day example I want to give is the story of a fervent Christian woman that I know. She was doing various kinds of work in the ministry. Early morning on a particular day, about 14-15 years ago, still at her Bible work and daily vocational ministry, she suddenly felt something struck her body, took her off the seat, and knocked her to the ground. And from that day onwards, she became paralyzed, though she was rushed to a hospital in Lagos and was there for one month with literally zero improvements.

After that, she was taken to Abeokuta, where she was placed in one position for 10 weeks, sleeping on the same posture. She couldn't be in a sitting posture; she could not walk, and so was passing out all her wastes on that same bed. She ate on the same bed, took her bath there, and did everything on a wooden bed for 10 weeks.

Soon, the nation-wide strike of the Medical Association of Nigeria made her to seek medical care elsewhere. She was flown to England and for one month, she could not see any specialist because she had no National ID number to get medical attention. So, after one month of being on the same spot, another door opened and she was flown to the US on a wheel chair.

It usually took her about 20 minutes to get out of a staircase that is not more than 10 feet. There was even a day that she was going to the hospital for another series of tests, as she was coming out of the train station with crutches on both hands, she couldn't go further because of the crowd; but all of a sudden, she heard a voice. At this time that she heard the voice, she saw nobody around. The voice said, "It is I who has brought you this far, and I will not desert you." From that day, healing started to take place in her life. Remember I said she fell off her chair when the incidence happened and lost her lumber bones 2 to 5. When she eventually began to receive medical treatments, the medical team wondered how she was still able to stand. "You should be permanently on wheel chair," they said. She went through series of surgeries, and prayers were being raised for her from all over the world where her friends were.

From the moment she heard God's voice, her healing began to take place. God's fullness of grace and mercy began to strengthen her; she trusted in the Lord, and continued to serve the Lord as much as she could from a pure heart. She continued to lay hold on her rights as a child of God, and the healing continued.

Afterwards, the Lord commissioned her, assuring her of total healing, and the Lord made her to see that, as she would be going about sharing this testimony, her healing would be perfected. God told her that as she laid hands on the sick and those under demonic attack, He would follow through with His Word.

This woman has been doing the work since that time, and I present to you that the same woman is the one sharing this with you. I can now stand on my two legs, speaking the word of God and sharing with the world a faithful God. Praise the Lord! The agony, the stress, the humiliation I went through would fill the pages of a whole book if I were to write them. It was God that got me through it all. I live in the US now—I was not the one that decided to relocate to the US. My ministry was going on very well in Nigeria, and all I cared about was to visit the US and the UK, not to live there. As I pastor the church of God in Queens, New York, God continues to reveal Himself to many.

Three Things You Must Note:

Firstly, serving God is a thing you must do from a clear and pure heart. If you really want to serve God, serve Him.

Secondly, as you serve Him, know that nothing shall by any means hurt you. Luke 10:19 says, "Behold, I have given you authority to tread on serpents and scorpions, and over all the power of the enemy, and nothing shall hurt you" (ESV).

Dearly beloved, that assurance is enough for me to go to places with the Gospel of Jesus Christ because I have personally experienced it.

And thirdly, I know that I have been commissioned to pray with and for you. I don't know the type of disease you have on your body, I don't know how long you've been suffering from it, if the Lord could heal my lumber bones, which meant a broken spinal cord, He can heal you. And I say that to the glory of God; be assured that He will heal you as well.

There's nothing God cannot do. Being bedridden for ten meant shame and humiliation for me, but God knew where He was taking me, and here I am speaking to you today. That's why during church services, I cannot do without dancing with the legs. People who came to America and saw my name on the newspaper advertising the church, knowing what happened to me were shocked, and they called to ask, "Are you still the one? What about those legs?" People who were visiting me for those 10 weeks in the hospital were peeling out my skin; they peeled out my skin on a particular day and filled a cup.

My dear, what can God not do? Do you have a story; everybody has a story. My own story is that Jesus saved me and healed me. Have you been saved? If you are not, then you need to consider what the Lord Jesus did for you on the Cross and consider accepting Him as the Lord of your life today. That's the beginning of it all, and it is the starting point for your blessings. And if you have been saved, you must understand that victory is already yours in Christ!

END of Sermon by Rev. Mrs. Regina Kehinde.

2

Your Free Gift—Grace

*H*ere is a major question from the sermon:
Have you asked Jesus to be the Lord of your
life? If you have not, here are a few notes and
scriptures to help you—some truths that you need to
know now:

- God created Adam and Eve to fellowship with
  Him. They had God's life in them and they could
  easily connect freely with Him (Genesis 2:7).

- When Adam and Eve sinned, we lost our connec-
  tion with God. Humans no longer had the capacity
  to be in tune with God (Genesis 3:8-10).

- Since man went against God's plan, choosing to
  make decisions for themselves, they handed over
  the control of their lives to Satan, who became
  human's new master and instructor. So evil began
  to rule over man (Psalm 81:12, Romans 8:7, John
  10:10).

❧ Therefore, sin became human's new nature replacing the godly nature—God's likeness (Galatians 5:17).

❧ The Laws came into the puzzle to get man to see that he could not do without the life of God that was in him at the beginning (Romans 7:7-25).

❧ Then, Jesus came to give us a brand new nature; He died so that anyone that accepts His work will have this new nature. Human beings now have access to a new kind of nature that can clothe them with God's likeness, and connect them freely with God (John 3:16, John 10:10, Romans 5:1-2, Romans 8:1-4).

❧ This new life was a free gift for everyone. It cost Jesus His throne in heaven and His life on earth. However, we got it free (Ephesians 1:7-10, Ephesians 2:8).

❧ Freedom becomes available to those that accept the new life in Christ. It's for those who confess their sins and accept that they were disconnected from God and long for reconnection with the Father (1 John 1:9, Romans 5:1-2, Colossians 2:13-15).

❧ They accept this gift of salvation by faith in the One who brought them to earth in the first place (Ephesians 2:8).

꩜ First, they realize that they were the ones running their own life, not their Maker; they accept that as much as they tried to be good by obeying some or all the laws, they still could not connect with God (Romans 7:7-25, 2 Corinthians 5:18-19).

꩜ Therefore, they realize that they need a savior, and then they accept the Lord Jesus as their Savior and the new master of their lives (Ephesians 2: 1-10, 1 Corinthians 5:17).

꩜ By faith, they accept that when Jesus died on the cross, they died to sin; and that when He rose back to life, they got the new life in Christ (Galatians 2:19-20, 2 Corinthians 5:17).

꩜ They forever enjoy their new life in God's new kingdom, that whether here on earth or up in heaven, they are at peace with God because of what the Lord Jesus did for them (John 3:16).

꩜ This new life is so rich. And so, they continue to discover each day, all that is included in this package of Grace (Colossians 2:1-23, Romans 12: 2).

꩜ Victory over sin and over every attempt of the enemy has been given to everyone who believes in Christ. However, not everyone enjoys that freedom and victory.

꩜ So my dear, these are reasons why Rev. Regina said in her sermon that your blessings started at the Cross. If you are now in tears, for one reason or the other, what you need to do first is to check where you stand as to salvation. If you are at the beginning of the process, please go ahead, step down from the throne of your life, and ask Jesus to take the place of the King and Lord of your life. Give Him your life now and receive His gift to you. Remember that you did not work for this gift—it's a gift. Thank Him for it and enjoy your gift.

After that, you will then need to discover all the blessings you already have in your hamper. This is one reason it's important to join a group of people that have received the new life, too. You will need to know more about your new life. Christ Himself through the Holy Spirit will reveal the truths to you on a daily basis. Therefore, the more of your rights that you discover, the more of your blessing you will receive, and then the more of it you will enjoy.

The truth is that the devil will not just look away and accept defeat from you, No! He will also fight back. So get ready. What you are going through now could even be part of his fight to get you to doubt God. Remember his full-time work is to tempt and trouble people.

John 10:10 says, *"The thief does not come except to steal, and to kill, and to destroy. I have come*

that they may have life, and that they may have it
more abundantly."

. . . .

. . . .

1 Peter 5:8 likewise says, "*Be sober-minded; be*
watchful. Your adversary the devil prowls around
like a roaring lion, seeking someone to devour."

. . . .

The wicked one will use anything he can to get you to
suffer. He will make efforts to take your health, your joy,
your hope, and even your faith in God. He will tell you
all sorts of lies just to get you to doubt God's promises
of love and hope.

You must focus on what God says and fight hard to hold
onto the truth of the word of God until you see it happen
for real. Don't take no for an answer. Say to yourself that
since the word of God says a thing, it means it's true,
though I am yet to experience it. Holy Spirit, please help
me to accept what God's word says as the truth (and
not what my experience is). Help me to hold onto your
word as the truth every day until my reality becomes
the same as what the truth is. At the later end of this
book, I have put a Scriptures Treasure Chest together for
you. You can start your faith work from there or make
it your go-to chest whenever you need to.

3

— Part Three —

Testimonials

Stories and testimonies written in the Bible continue to help many today. Here are a few testimonies of present-day believers. We have prayerfully compiled them for you to see that God is the same yesterday and forever.

The enemy is out to render Generals like you powerless, for his full-time job is to discourage comrades and make them weak. However, with our testimonies, we overcame.

Rev 12:11 ESV —

. . . .

And they have conquered him by the blood of the Lamb and by the word of their testimony, for they loved not their lives even unto death.

. . . .

God of All Possibilities

By Rotimi Odekeye

ndeed, there are no impossibilities with God. There is no sickness or disease that God cannot heal. There is no prayer that is wasted as long as it's based on His revealed will for us, His children. God always desires to heal.

It all happened far back in 2011, on 4 January, when my wife gave birth to our first daughter, Anjola-Oluwa. In the process of the childbirth, she lost so much blood that there was a need for blood transfusion. As the first point of call, I was asked to donate a pint of blood, so I quickly rushed to the laboratory to do just that. On getting there, my blood sample was taken for some clinical tests to ascertain its viability. To my surprise, I was told I wouldn't be able to donate since the result showed that I had Hepatitis (a liver condition that affects the blood).

At first, I was not seriously bothered because I did not know anything about it, but I guessed it would be something worth attending to urgently, since it disqualified me from undergoing the blood donation. Fortunately, we got another donor for my wife as needed, and God took all the glory in that part of our life. But as for the new discovery, I began to seek for understanding concerning this blood condition.

I met with an experienced family nurse who could not but mince words and stammer while explaining, for she would not want to do what is referred to as damage in the medical world. There and then, I knew there was more to this condition than what I thought. Eventually, I got to know that it was a deadly condition that should be managed with medication, which I took for sometimes and then stopped, as I became angry in my spirit. I decided to trust in God, the great Physician.

The adventure (trusting in God) started with engaging the power of prayer and faith in the healing power that God has made available to us (His children) through the shed blood of Jesus Christ. I must say that having God's people around us whom we could confide in and who joined us in prayers was of paramount importance, as the scripture says that, the prayers of the righteous (ones) avail much. I really enjoyed that concerted anointing from brothers and sisters in Christ. Only God could reward their labour of love.

Series of spiritual activities were embarked on, ranging from sowing seeds to attending special healing services, even though I could not ascertain the scriptural truth around sowing a seed (giving an offering to get healing). However, God proved Himself as a faithful Father.

My wife called me one day, after we had believed God for a while, and said, "Man of God! You have exercised your faith so far, it is time you went to do a test to establish the testimony." I agreed it was time to for medical tests.

Confusion was written all over our faces (lab scientist and myself) when he could not ascertain the reality of the previous test after conducting the test this time. Again, my blood sample was taken for a superior lab scientist to conduct the test for a second time, but the same confusion lingered, meaning that the blood condition was nowhere to be found. I am bold to say that, since then, I have had no cause to visit the hospital as I have enjoyed divine health so far.

One thing I know, this experience has shifted my faith level to a higher level, to believe God for anything in the area of healing, and I know that God, who did it for me, is still in the business of healing. He will heal all of your diseases and sicknesses.

Praise God!

Rotimi Odekeye, *he is a lover of God, with a sweet loving wife and 2 wonderful daughters. One thing he desires is to see all around him come to the knowledge of God through the revealed word. He lives in Abuja, Nigeria.*

He has a Plan

by Joshua Ilondior

My name is Joshua, born and raised in Lagos. I went to the Federal University of Technology (FUTO), Owerri, for my tertiary education and I was posted to the Northern part of Nigeria, Kano State for my youth service (NYSC). The trip there was a hectic one. It took us almost two days to drive from Lagos to Kano because the roads were bad, and there were armed robbers on the way. We had to divert after getting a hint from drivers coming from opposite side of traffic. We saw various accidents and narrowly escaped one; it was such a stressful experience.

After this ordeal, I vowed not to travel by road back to Lagos, and I was determined to do everything it might cost me to travel by air. I began to save towards my flight ticket after doing research on the cost. As at this time in my life, I had never been on an airplane, and it was going to be my first flight. I refused to take holidays or go back home during the short breaks and the Christmas holiday because I really needed to save enough for the trip.

During my last week of service at my NYSC place of assignment, I felt led by God to sow my ticket money to help others in the upcoming NYSC batch. At that time, I was the president of my fellowship. I struggled with the thought for a day, considering all the efforts I had made to raise the money, but I finally gave in. I put down all the tens of thousands of my hard-earned, saved money. I had this strong conviction that if I would board a plane back to Lagos, I would not be the one to pay for it. One thing led to another and I ended up traveling by road, but my conviction did not wane.

My testimony here is that after spending exactly one month in Lagos with my family, I got a call from an American-based NGO in Abuja to work for them. The organization paid for my flight ticket, and this marked my first time of traveling in a plane. Thereafter, I traveled to about three African countries by air and not a dime was spent from my pocket for the tickets. Now, I live and work in the US and even my flight to the US as well was fully paid for. I have since traveled to three continents and I can say that most of those times, I didn't pay for the tickets.

God is faithful and He sees the hearts of man. We can never out give God.

Joshua Ilondior *was born into a family of 4 boys. His family originated from the souther part of Nigeria called Delta State.*

After trainng to be an Engineer, he picked up some certifications in computer networking and cabling. He also did trainin I under several Pastors in Nigeria, Canada, and the US. He has been involved with short time mission trips with about 6 countries within 3 continents. He is a peoples person who loves to serve others. He has worked in serveral companies within Nigeria and the US. He also runs his own company with a vision to impact his world. Most of his spare time he loves to spend with his wife and two lovely daughters.

God's Providence in our Wedding

by Anonymous

My wife and I agreed to get married before we both proceeded to higher institutions. While my wife studied in Nigeria, I studied in the United States of America. As a result, our courtship lasted for six years before we got married. Within these years, we set out some days for prayers and fasting concerning God's providence on our plans for a successful wedding and our marriage life.

After my completing my studies, I came back to Nigeria to do one-year National Youth Service Corps (NYSC) program. I made some savings towards our marriage (traditional and wedding) during the NYSC period. I used to deposit the savings on a monthly basis with my fiancée then, now my wife. At the end of the NYSC, we had the traditional marriage, which was quite successful with very few leftovers. At this point, we had just three hundred naira left from our savings for the wedding. Meanwhile, as to our wedding preparation, we had no wedding gown, reception venue, refreshment items, and accommodation; and worst still, I had no job. Therefore, we sent prayer points to some Christian friends to join us in prayer concerning those challenges. With all these challenges before us, we went ahead to print and distribute our wedding invitation cards in less than two months to the set date.

My fiancée then had just started her internship as a pharmacist. We had set out days and times to meet, pray, and evaluate progress towards a successful wedding. One fateful day, she visited me from her place of work. I sensed in my spirit that something had gone wrong for her to visit at such a time. While she was yet to disclose the reason for her visit, a friend and his wife drove into my compound to visit, too. Seeing us together, they thanked God for meeting the two of us at the same time. None of these visits were scheduled—both theirs and my fiancée's. Without wasting much time, they went straight to disclose the purpose of their visit. They had received our prayer points and God ministered to them to fund everything concerning the reception refreshment up to the grain of salt. The couple asked for the list and quantity of each item, the venue, and the date to deliver those items. Both of us were dumbfounded at such offer. It was like a dream. We thanked them for such a kind gesture and pleaded with them to allow us buy the drinks. At this time, I was still counting on the balance of three hundred naira to assist them with drinks because a crate of soft drinks was still four naira then. They reluctantly accepted our plea. They then prayed with us and left. It was after they left that my fiancée disclosed the reason for her unscheduled visit. When she got back home from work, she could not find the three hundred naira she kept. I had to persuade her not to be bothered by that because the sum of money was nothing compared with the offer we received from the couple. God must have arranged both her visit and that of the couple.

Now, we were left with arranging for drinks, the reception venue, the wedding gown, and where to live after marriage. Don't forget; I was still jobless at this time. As the date was drawing very close, we made some enquiry about where we could get enough empty crates (about 25 crates) to enable us place order for drinks. We were told of another Christian couple who happened to be friends as well. When we approached them to request for the empty crates, we received another amazing offer from them. They gave us crates full of drinks, which were more than enough for the wedding reception, for free!

Getting a venue for our reception was another miracle. With the intervention of God, we were given a furnished, easily accessible hall free of charge.

The wedding gown miraculously arrived on Wednesday, just three days to the wedding, from the United States of America. About two weeks before then, my wife's elder sister had offered to amend hers, as she was quite fatter than my wife was. Even though we had lost communication with her for a long time, she was able to get in touch with us.

In all, we had a very successful wedding with surplus for the entertainment of our guests. We had a live Christian band that played at no cost, and all who travelled from afar returned safely to their respective destinations on that same day. And the Lord blessed us with fantastic weather—no sun, no rain—everything was just cool.

The wedding came to pass successfully. We did not owe anybody anything at a time when working people would get married and still pile up a huge debt after their wedding ceremonies. In fact, we had cash gifts! After the wedding, we travelled to Lagos for our honeymoon. While on honeymoon, I got an employment. God miraculously met our need for accommodation, again at no cost to us!

Indeed, we have experienced and can testify that God is a present help in time of need.

If He said it, He will do it

by Oluwatobiloba Moody

This testimony is about God's faithfulness and His ability to do what He promised, in spite of situations, which seem to indicate otherwise. I graduated with an LLM distinction from the University of Western Cape, South Africa, and reflecting on the journey, I could say it's nothing short of a miracle.

I had been working with a medium-sized law firm. Though I was getting good reviews, I really felt within that there was more that I was meant to be doing. It was as though there was a call to something deeper. I prayed about it and really felt that it was important for me to pursue my master's degree in a specialized field. I had applied to a school in South Africa, which offered the specialized degree (the first of its kind in Africa), but I heard nothing back from the institution.

I felt as though I was in a limbo, and for a while, I just continued prodding on.

In a point of desperation, I decided one day to fast and pray. I really wanted to wait on the Lord get a sense of His direction for me. After work that day, I took a walk to the sports center, just praying and meditating. As I sat down alone in the stands, and began to read my Bible, the Lord led me to Psalm 22 verse 21. As I read it, it literally jumped out at me. I saw myself in the Psalm, and was filled with hope like never before. A particular phrase stuck me—"and He answered me." It was surreal, but from that point, I was so sure that the Lord had heard me and that I would be commencing my masters. The reality seemed otherwise though. The date that had been indicated for the school to get back to successful candidates had long passed. I still waited, hoping and trusting to receive a reply. I later resigned from my job, still having not heard anything from the school. When asked about the cause of my resignation, I informed my boss that I wanted to prepare for my resumption for a master's program. It was all a statement of faith.

As I stayed at home daily, I began to spend more time in prayer. Sincerely, by this time, I was already lining up possible alternatives, as several thoughts ran through my mind — 'Probably God had actually decided otherwise for me, or maybe I misunderstood

His message.' One morning as I was praying, I sensed the Lord asking me to stop the prayers, pick my phone, and call the school I had applied to. I first hesitated. Eventually, I called and, for the first time, was able to get through to the program coordinator. She told me what I had suspected that, the admission cycle had been concluded and I had not been selected. I thanked her and dropped the phone. As I resumed my prayers, I began asking the Lord, "What should be my next step now?" I heard Him asking me to call her once again and, this time, ask if I could sponsor myself on the program (the program was a scholarship-based one for which admitted candidates were offered funding). This time again, I really hesitated, as it was clear I had not been accepted for the program. I didn't want to be insulted.

After a little thought, I succumbed and called her again. This time, it was as though I was speaking to someone different. We conversed for a while, and I asked about the possibility of sponsoring myself on the program. She then reviewed my application while speaking with me, and was impressed with it. She explained that she'd place my application on top of the wait list in case any of those who had been offered admission turned their spots down. One person declined this offer. Some days later, I was offered admission to the program.

That was the beginning of a remarkable academic journey that was God's favor for me. During the program, I enjoyed God's grace and excelled by His Spirit at work in me. I graduated with distinctions and, through the program, found myself strategically positioned for a career in line with the vision that had been placed in my heart. I remain eternally grateful to the Lord.

Oluwatobiloba Moody is from Egbe, in Kogi State of Nigeria. He is a lawyer by training and is married to Abisoye. They have a little daughter, Anjoreoluwa. Tobi is currently studying for his PhD in Canada and, in his spare time, he enjoys baking, playing music and playing basketball. He loves God

He's Got Your Back

by Abi Kunle Olowosoyo

This happened to me, I think, in August 2000. I had been on a job for about three months as a sales assistant for a major UK national photography equipment company, and my store was located in central London.

I did my best on the job despite the challenges I had regarding getting to work early, every morning. The journey could have been shorter if I took some other means of transport, but I could only afford to travel by bus. Yet I was never late and I always made big sales, which even made some of my contemporaries jealous sometimes.

While on a weekend duty one day with the store manager, about four teenagers came into the store and hiding under the busy atmosphere of the store, they managed to force open one of the glass shelves where very expensive equipment were kept. The teens, three boys and a girl stole an expensive camera and went away unnoticed.

When the theft was discovered, the police was called in but there was no way they could trace the thieves. Though the teens made a small purchase in the store, we found they paid with a stolen credit card. There was a proof of forced entry on the glass shelf, but my company blamed me because I was the last person to sell an equipment from the shelf. I was called to a meeting within the week and got sacked. This was so demoralizing because I put in so much in that job.

When I got home, I had a prayer session with my wife wherein I told God how I felt about my job loss, and we prayed for a better job within one week. I was dismissed on a Friday and by Wednesday the following week; I was in my first job in the construction industry. Not only was I being paid nearly twice as what I got in the previous job, the new job also opened a new chapter for me in a new industry. This led to another appointment with a new employer who retrained me as a Quantity Surveyor, with all expenses paid for me. Now I work as a Contracts Manager for a construction company.

A few weeks after my dismissal, I was in central London with my wife and thought I would go and say hello to my old colleagues. I was surprised to find my old store had been closed down. God will fight your corner when you can't and He also sees further and can position you above the storm. Finally, God makes all things work together for our good.

Abi Kunle Olowosoyo is a child of God and a minister of the Gospel at Harmony Christian Centre, Harold Wood, London. Married to Abiola and they are blessed with two sons.

Secured in Him

by T.R

We relocated in 2015 and started to trust the Lord for a permanent job when I completed an internship in February. The prospects looked tough, with job losses around, and I was even advised to move to another area of the country, as my preferred field was not 'in demand' where I was.

My husband and I agreed in prayer to trust God to give us our desire before the end of April, and we had a word of confirmation from our Pastor that we should focus on being close to God and trust Him to open a way.

To the glory of God, in the second week of April, I got a permanent job after successfully completing an interview that started with 400 candidates.

Thank you, T.R.

If God Be For Me

by Anonymous

O n an early Tuesday morning while parking my car at my workplace, I found myself being surrounded by Canada Border Service Agency (CBSA). The officers told me that I was not allowed to be in the country. Immediately, I was struck with fear and confusion. I thought within me, 'After studying for two year and working at a full-time job and even starting my very own business, how is this possible? Why now?' In a matter of minutes, I was handcuffed and detained on the count that I did not declare my past conviction to the immigration officer back in my home country and that I lied and so was living in Canada illegally. Then it hit me; my past had finally caught up on me, as I tried to explain why I came and how I managed to immigrate to the country, after losing my first family to the earthquake that took everything from me, and that I needed to escape the devastation.

I thought that they would understand, and someone would hear me out, but my cries were ignored. To the arresting officer, this was not his concern, and was not acceptable, since his job was to find the truth and deport illegal immigrants.

I came to realize later that God was gracious to me, but I was doing things my way. To be a Christian and live a lie is a great offence, and I clearly understood that I lied and was out of the will of God for my life. I sat down, made everything very clear, and was completely honest as I repented of my wrongdoing in the sight of God. I was held and awaited trial from the immigration board.

During this time, I was incarcerated; something I swore would never happen to me again. When things started to look worse, God, on the other hand, was working, not only on the officer's heart but also with the leaders of my local church, who supported my family and me. The love that was shown to my family was far beyond what I had expected. Sometimes, we usually look for some huge sign to know God is working for us, but I found out that God was working through my wife and pastors and his family, not to mention others who were praying for me all over the world.

While I was behind bars, I kept on reading my Bible and praying, and God opened the doors wherein I had the opportunity to lead a young man to Christ. Then, the third day came when I had to stand trial before a judge, and after the court hearing on whether I was eligible to remain in Canada or not, the judge found me inadmissible. Then the next decision was on whether I should be detained or released. The prosecuting officer proposed that a bond should be set at $7500, but grace stepped in when the judge objected that it was too high, and ruled that I should be released with the bond set at $3000. Within few hours, my pastor posted the bond, and I was released in the evening. Things could have gotten a lot worse, not only for me but also for my family if God's grace had not prevailed for me even though I was wrong. Despite my disobedience, He remained faithful.

Currently, my family and I have applied for refugee status and we clearly believe that God is working on our behalf as we wait for an answer, whatever it may be. One thing is certain, God is with us, and we are highly favored, for we know that all things work together for those that love God, and are called to His purpose.

My prayer is, as you read this, you will be able to see God's hands in everything. Where we were underserving of His love and grace, yet He loved us even more; where we were underserving of His goodness, His grace abounded more.

Google defines grace as (in Christian belief) the free and unmerited favor of God, as manifested in the salvation of sinners and the bestowal of blessings. The more I examine my life, the more I see myself as a man to whom God has abundantly been graceful. From my 12-year sentence and serving six years, I often heard the same words, "My grace is sufficient for you." From being deported from the US to arriving at my homeland, and having a chance to raise a family, I heard the word again, "My grace is sufficient for you." From raising a family and later losing them to the 2010 earthquake, I heard the Lord, "My grace is sufficient for you." From migrating to Canada to study, heading back home to get married to a wonderful woman, and to receiving the blessing of two beautiful Canadian-born children, God still said, "My grace is sufficient for you."

From the word of Paul, I found a solace— "what shall we say to these things, if God be for me, who can be against me" (Romans 8:31).

God wants us to know that even in our mistakes, He loves us totally, with an everlasting love, and He is able to make all things work together for our good.

I Will Give You Rest!

By Jean Yves Ntone

long with a group of friends, I decided to attend the opening service of one of our branches, located in a city, approximately a three-hour drive away from where I lived and rented a car for the occasion. On the day of our departure, things did not go according to the plan, we left two hours later than anticipated, which made me disappointed and irritated. Being time-conscious, I could barely control myself while, on the contrary, all the other passengers in the car were relaxed and ready for a weekend of celebration.

As the assigned driver that day, I was looking for a way to reach our destination as early as possible. The only idea that came to mind was to increase the speed in order to cut the lost time in half. As I cruised on the highway that day, my only wish was to be on one of the highways in Germany where there are no speed limits.

As I accelerated, driving above the allowed speed limits, a thought crossed my mind to handover the steering wheel to the person who was seated next to me, an experienced and careful driver. I quickly dismissed the idea as a silly one and followed through with the plan to over-speed and, at the same time, I disregarded the signs reminding drivers of the hefty penalties that the authority could met out to careless drivers. I was hoping that luck would be on my side as it was the case in my previous attempts.

On two occasions, cars that were in front slowed me down, and this aggravated me. The other passengers in the car pressed me to slow down, but I ignored their plea. I was determined to drive fast for us to be at our destination as quickly as possible.

There is a rule in baseball dubbed, "Three strikes and you're out." While on the road, I got warned three times but didn't listen. Little did I know that luck was on my side that day. Halfway through the journey, a police car flushed from behind, and before long, I received my first ticket for offensive driving. Things got complicated when I learned that our car would have to be towed as well. I did not pay attention to the road sign that any vehicle exceeding the allowed speed limit by 50 km/h would automatically be towed.

My world was crushed down. We were in the middle of nowhere! The police officer was kind enough to call a taxi for us, which was another unplanned expense. The silence in that car was deafening. I could tell that my friends were utterly disappointed by the poor and dangerous decision I had taken that evening.

As a result, my driver's license got suspended for ten days, and I had to pay for the towing fees as well as the rental fees of the taxi during the suspension period. I was served a notice to appear in court to determine what my actual fine would be, which normally starts at $10000. Besides, I still had to figure out how to get back home following the event. It was a hefty price to pay for the oversight and negligence!

The storm was unbearable, and I simply could not take it anymore! The pit I started digging by my decision to over speed now seemed too deep, I was literally sinking, and there was nowhere to find comfort or someone to encourage me, except God.

With the little knowledge I had of Him, I started reflecting on how He had changed the lives of many characters in the Bible whose problems seemed similar to mine in the sense that they lost hope at a point in their lives. I had read about Bible characters like David and the adulterous woman, and discovered how they got a second chance in their own lives, which was all I needed—a second chance.

After moments of introspection, I realized that my anger blinded my decision-making process so much that I overlooked the deadly consequences of my own actions. My reckless driving could have killed my friends, other road users, or me. The realization of God's mercy and protection was His seal and confirmation of a second chance to me.

As the court day approached, I became nervous. Some part of me believed God for a miracle but another did not want to set high expectations. On the day of the hearing, I witnessed the divine intervention of God. When the judge called out my name and discovered I was driving at 153 KM/h, he asked the prosecutor if they could do something for me considering the fact that my driving report was clean as of that time. He suggested that they should instead register on the court documents that I was driving at 149 KM/h, which translated in a penalty of $350 instead of over $10,000. It was a miracle I had been waiting for. I could not contain my excitement. I immediately texted my relatives saying, "He (Jesus) did it!"

The whole experience cost me around $2000, but it was nothing compared to the load I felt was removed from my shoulders. From that day, I can relate to this passage in the Bible: *"Come to Me, all you who labor and are heavy laden, and I will give you rest"* (Matthew 11:28 NKJV).

__Jean Yves Ntone__ is a mechanical engineer by profession and a former employee of Air France in Montreal. He enjoys building people and working to advance the Body of Christ. He has been serving in the leadership team at Overcomers Assembly since 2006. He is currently the resident pastor of the Montreal West branch. He is married to Rose Wangechi, and the Lord has blessed them with a beautiful girl.

It was then that I carried you!

By Anonymous

As we journey through life, we face many trials along the way. One of the many trials I faced was when the company wherein I've worked for ten years decided to close their Montreal office. I was working for this company from home and was quite comfortable with the job. Being able to work from home gave me a good work-life balance.

I was an expert at what I did and I was in my comfort zone. I did not receive a reasonable severance package after I was laid off. Having been faithful to the company for ten years and having invested ten years of my life keeping their customers satisfied, I felt that I was mis-treated. Being a single mother of a college student, I had to redouble my efforts to find a new job. We were given a four-month notice, and I was working during the day and looking for a job for a night shift. Although the company promised affected staff some job search assistance, nothing was provided. I went to several interviews and although they went well, it seemed like nothing was coming through.

I would like to step aside and diverge from my narrative for a moment. I frequently say, "This is no garden of Eden" to imply that life will not always be rosy. Most times, while we are sailing on calm seas, the enemy stirs up a storm. We see that as Peter stepped out of the boat to walk on water. The wind was contrary and as he got his eyes off Jesus, he began to sink. While sailing through life in high, tempestuous wind, we become tempted to focus on the circumstances and get our eyes off Jesus. We need to refocus and keep our eyes fixed on the Author and Finisher of our faith. It is easy for the enemy to whisper in your ear, "You're going to sink, for there is no way out of this storm. Jesus is not coming to the rescue." However, when we refocus our vision on Jesus, He always reaches out and pulls us out of the stormy seas of life.

Now back to my narrative, finally, an opening came by in the way of a job offer with a better pay and more advancement opportunities. The Lord opened up a door for me to work from home again. It was not all bright and rosy, as the new job was not without its challenges; and I did not feel I was not in my usual comfort zone.

However, I could see now in hindsight, looking back at my footprints in the sand, the tough times had only one set of footprints and in the words of the Lord, 'It was then that I carried you.' In closing, remember what the book of Romans says, "*All things work together for good for them that love God and are called according to His purpose.*"

Power of Prayers

By Fern Bath

I married a gospel minister who had lost his wife to cancer at the age of 36 and left him with four children all under 14 years of age. I had never been married before, so this was a big change for me. Although I had been teaching and working with all ages in the Province of New Found Land, being a mother to the kids wasn't a problem to me, but naturally, we wanted to have a child of our own. It took four years into the marriage before we had a son.

This was pretty exciting to my husband's oldest son because he already had three sisters but no brothers. Then when our son took terribly ill, we were devastated. He was only 18 months at the time and seemed so helpless. I had noticed while changing his diaper, his stools were very black, very abnormal. My babysitter at the time was a well-seasoned mother herself, while I was teaching the Kindergarten class. She informed us that the little boy was quite sick, so we rushed him to the hospital as an emergency. We felt he might have the Rae's disease, which could leave him mentally retarded, or cause his death. The doctors and nurses could not bring his fever down, and we were not allowed to hold him because of his high body temperature. He would cry for us to pick him up, but we couldn't. It was too heartbreaking for us that we were not supposed to cuddle our 18-month-old baby, who had already lost half of the body fat and protein, and his liver was enlarged.

When the medical workers felt they could no longer manage the boy's condition, they decided to take him by ambulance to the sick children's hospital in St. Johns, which was a 4-hour drive from where we lived. When we knew how stressful it would be for him to be transported by ambulance that distance, we wept and cried till we arrived the hospital. We needed a miracle from God.

We know that "Prayer changes things," and we had everyone everywhere praying all over the nation. They put our son on a cooling blanket right away to get the fever down as much as possible, to avoid the possibility of brain damage. He was in isolation in the hospital; we had to wear gowns when visiting, and could finally hold him again. It was so hard to see his little eyes sunken back into his head, as he looked so pale and weak and helpless. Each day, his condition improved; and after 9 days, he was discharged from the hospital on a special diet—no dairy but a soy-based formula—which he did not like. He had to learn how to regain his strength and walk again. He was wobbling and weak on his little feet.

We cannot thank God enough because when the specialist said they had ruled out the Rae's syndrome disease, we felt a relief.

We could feel the force of prayer breaking through the barrier to restore health to our son; God honored the faith of church members that gave themselves to fasting and praying.

We are thankful to God who is concerned about our every situation in life, and nothing is too small or too large for Him to solve. He just wants us to trust Him and understand His power—what He can do. Today, our son is 6 feet tall and a gifted musician, who can play almost any instrument and has a precious little daughter. We trust God who can turn the tables, and is concerned about every area of our lives.

Fern Bath lives in Kingston, Ontario. She had her degree in Bible and Theology. Met her husband: Rev Bath while teaching in Newfoundland. They both served the Lord in many capacities such as church planting and pastoring community churches around NewFoundland and Ontario. They are blessed with children, grand children that are servicing God all over the world. She and her husband continue to support ministers to continue in the work of the father. She is passionate about praying for others.

He Is My Everything!

By Oluwaseun Adesina

I had always thought I was a good girl until an encounter in secondary school, which revealed to me who I really was and how I needed someone to help me live the way I ought.

I attended a boarding secondary school in Nigeria. We had returned to school from our holidays at the time and, of course, everyone was very excited to share their holiday experiences but something struck me about a friend of mine. Her story was somewhat different from the rest of us. She seemed to have discovered a kind of treasure and she was definitely very passionate about what she had found! I also noticed she radiated a "newness" that you would not miss in her conversation and mannerism.

One day, she asked if we could attend an event that was taking place in our school but was organized by some students from a nearby University. I heard about the impact of the event and decided to go with my friends.

The organizers were very warm and pleasant, and you could see "something" from inside out about them, which was subtle, yet extremely powerful. They prayed for some of the students who were already infected by a strange outbreak that made their legs to be shaking involuntarily. During the event, some of them actually got healed! However, it was the pure message of everyone's need for a savior, no matter their age, color, gender, or race that impacted me most. The speaker spoke of many things I could relate with and the fact that God had already made provision through His Son for me to overcome the world of sin. I realized that I was not as "good" as I thought I was. In fact, I realized I could never be on my own, that God was waiting for me to allow Him into my heart so He could help me navigate this wilderness called *life* by standing on my side. It was as though a big burden I was trying to carry on my own was taken away and I had a new wave of peace I had never experienced before.

Consequently, I began to know God in many ways apart from being my Savior. There have been various challenges but through diverse ups-and-downs, God remains constant.

I recall an experience I had wherein I needed some funding to complete my professional examinations in Accounting. I did not have enough to pay for one of the modules of the examination and I did not know what to do. I remember crying and walking on Anthony Bridge in Lagos on my way home one day, not minding if anyone was looking, and I was asking if God had forgotten me. Eventually, as God would have it, my sister's husband (her fiancé at the time) gave me the money. I became a chartered accountant and thereafter, became a Finance Manager in an IT company.

Another challenge arose when I got married and for some reason, I could not get pregnant! I fasted and prayed, but nothing happened. I even took some medical tests that were excruciating. While praying one day, I heard the words, "I will make everything beautiful in my time" and I realized God was going to do it but only at the time He wanted—and that made me cry even more! I even resigned from my job with the hope that I would be able to "rest" better and so get pregnant sooner. I assumed that the pressure at my workplace was preventing me from getting pregnant since the medical tests were all good. After staying home for six months without working and not getting pregnant, I started re-applying for work and decided I would be of service to God even if I don't eventually have children. I had allowed my situation to overwhelm me to the point that everything else was going downhill and I had even forgotten what God had told me while praying—and that God does not lie!

My husband and I started making plans to relocate outside of Nigeria. I first started working again in a telecommunications company and then moved to a consulting firm. I stopped making the issue of not having children my priority, though I was still praying to God for help and mercy.

One day, while at work, I was feeling so tired that one of my colleagues told me visit the hospital for some tests. I was shocked when I was told that I was PREGNANT! It seemed unreal; so I did another test on my own and the results confirmed that I was still PREGNANT! I was four months pregnant when I relocated outside Nigeria and had my first son in the United States and the second in Canada (as we now live in Canada).

I will never forget God's goodness; and I feel my life only truly started the day I allowed God to become my Teacher, my Friend, my Guide, my Helper, my Confidant (I try to tell Him everything), my Strength, my Savior, my EVERYTHING...!

Oluwaseun is a Nigerian-Canadian. She's married and blessed with two boys. She holds an Accounting degree and is a Chartered Accountant. She's served in various roles such as Accounting clerk, Finance Manager, Head of Billing, Financial controls and Bid Administrator. She has worked on diverse youth projects over the years. These experiences have humbled her and increased her passion for children and youth evangelism. She composes Christian songs, and helps to coordinate the choir at her local church. She enjoys reading, listening to Christian music, and watching Christian movies.

Come As You Are

By Anonymous

For a long time, I have been among Christians. I was born into a Christian home, my parents loved God, and I attended church every Sunday with the family. Christianity essentially surrounded me. I had learned several scriptures over time, and if you asked me a Christian question, I definitely had the Christian answer for it or something close. Eventually, I figured if I could only appear Christian enough, I would be able to thrive with these people. So I learned how to pray from listening to others' prayer, I learned how to fake a divine encounter—the fidgeting, and falling under the influence of an unseen power. I regurgitated what was being fed me by this community of believers, and I could explain it all intelligently and logically. I was doing well for myself, or so I thought.

When I was nine, I lost my father. He was murdered. I was too young to form an intimate relationship with him. Though I mourned him, I didn't really understand what had happened. So many great stories were told about him, and it appeared he was a great guy, but I didn't know much of that for myself. I grew into a man without any real knowledge of what having a father was like. So this subliminally added to my indifference whenever the pastor would say things like, "God is a loving Father." I didn't have anything to relate it with, so it didn't mean much to me.

But in my heart, I wanted to believe there was someone out there watching over me. I didn't totally believe that I was alone, and just from seeing how things worked out in my family after my dad's passing, I knew there had to be a God out there who cared about us. Miraculously, my family didn't crumble to the ground, all my siblings went on to school and finished well, and eventually so did I. We got scholarships, God helped my mother, and all our needs were provided for somehow!

I can't quite say there was one magical day when it all just made sense, and God's love became so clear before my eyes. But reminiscing, I can honestly say that I now have an idea of what it's like to have a father who loves me. I'm not fatherless! I'm now more aware than ever that God is real, and God cares, even a thousand times more than an earthly father. I asked God to be Lord over my life five years ago, and even though there have been some roadblocks along the way, He's just always made a way out for me. I have no regrets whatsoever for consciously choosing this path. I have learned and I'm still learning to trust God more and more every day, because He knows the best for me, and He loves us.

Please, don't think that you have to impress Him to earn His good graces. He knows how messed up you are or will ever be, yet He accepts and loves you just the way you are, flaws and all. Come as you are and let God show you what a good and caring Father He is. You really don't have to struggle through life when your father is God. Wouldn't you rather live at peace, knowing that not just anyone, but God's got your back?

My Source and My Lord

by Victor Taiwo

My dad once worked in a bank, and we lived in affluence—at least, I remembered, we never lacked anything. Though he later went into businesses, some of which were bakery and eatery, they didn't do so well before he died of Typhoid Fever; that was when I had just got admitted into JSS1 (first year in high school). Nevertheless, we never lacked, as mum was there to take care of us kids, extended family members living with us, as well as family friends who usually came over when school was on holidays.

She worked at Fan Milk PLC, a major dairy firm, but later resigned to start a business, which was very successful. I remember in those days, she used to keep her money in cartons, as she was really a moneymaker; but all of a sudden, she was duped, and the business crumbled.

That was about six years after dad's death. Things got so bad that on the day I was to write my final exam in high school, which was Yoruba (a Nigerian language, which is also mine), we didn't have any money I could use for transport to the exam venue. After much delay, I got some money but I got there really late. I had A's, B's and C's in other courses while I got a P7 in Yoruba, which was the worst of my grades.

Well, that was just the beginning. I got an admission into one of the best Nigerian universities, OAU at my first attempt. By God's providence, I became a student of Engineering Physics, but my mum couldn't finance me any longer. My grandma tried her best, but the money she gave me each week was just enough to eat for barely 2 days. So after my first semester in school, I was in probation because I couldn't concentrate, I tried working on a menial job while on campus. I was selling bread and egg, and later took a leave of absence from school but eventually after about two years, I dropped out.

Before leaving secondary school, I had decided to follow Jesus Christ and His word totally, so I started attending a Bible-believing Church called Christ Way Church. When I got to OAU, I quickly joined a campus fellowship called Evangelical Christian Union where I could grow further in my faith. Later, with some friends, I started Christ Way Campus Fellowship in the name of my home church. By then I have met some Christian friends and some spiritual parents who took interest in me and encouraged me to get back to school. On that note, I wrote another exam and got an admission to study Computer Science with Mathematics at the Federal University of Agriculture, Abeokuta. Miraculously, my parents in Christ gave me financial support all through till I graduated with a B.Sc.

I am really grateful to God for helping me to know and follow Jesus and for sending other followers of Christ to me, to support me in my trying times. I'm forever grateful to all who supported me all through university and at those trying times. I wouldn't be married to my beautiful wife and have our lovely children and a happy home if I had not been able to go back to school by God's unusual provision. As of today, I won't be making a good amount of money from web development, public speaking, and computer sales and services, and, at the same time, be an educated, well-respected pastor, if it has not been God on my side. I would have been consumed with life challenges but God helped me. *"The young lions do lack, and suffer hunger: but they that seek the Lord shall not want any good things"* Psalm 34:10.

Victor Taiwo *started following Jesus Christ fully in 1994. He had an encounter with Christ through the testimony of an open vision his friend had. He was discipled and trained as a preacher of the word of truth and faith in Christ Jesus under Rev. Gbenga Olowosoyo, and Pastor Dr. Odun Orioke, the General Overseer of Christ Way Ministries International where he has been a lead pastor at three youth churches in the space of about 7 years with outstanding growth. Victor Taiwo was called by the Lord Jesus Christ to set the captives free through publishing of God's word in diverse and strategic ways. He is a passionate preacher and teacher of God's word, a counselor, life coach, and a healing and deliverance minister. He is a graduate of Computer Science with Mathematics, and has been a practicing entrepreneur. He founded SIP consulting, an ICT consulting firm in Ile-Ife, with an online presence. He is an ICT skills empowerment coach. He is married to Aderonke Taiwo, the host of "Love Talk with Ronke on YouTube" and "Scintillating Sex in Marriage," an NLP practitioner, public speaker, therapist and relationship coach. They are blessed with two children, Inioluwa and Ifeoluwa.*

Comfort in Christ and Consolation

By Dr. Mrs Helen Njoku

My name is Dr. Mrs. Helen C. Njoku, a pastor by the grace of God and also a proprietor of a school in Port Harcourt, Rivers State of Nigeria. I'married to Rev. Basil Sunday, and our marriage is blessed with seven children, five girls and two boys, to the glory of God. We are a happy family by the grace of God, serving the Lord in our own capacity, with the aim of accomplishing a purpose for the kingdom of God.

In January of 1997, our first son took ill while my husband was away in London, England. Just two days after he came back from his trip, the boy passed away on the 20th of the same month.

My whole life was devastated as though the world had collapsed on me. I was so confused, perplexed, and disappointed. It all happened as if it was a horrible dream, despite the fact that I had strong faith that my son would not die. But my faith shook when I heard the sound of my beloved son's breath whistling. I looked at the doctor, and a message of death was written on his face. I quickly refused it and demanded that they should allow the blood transfusion to continue, of which he obliged.

When I saw my 15-year-old son lying lifeless, I screamed, "How can this life waste? How can I loose such a boy with multi-faceted gifts? How could I ever part with him?" My husband dashed out immediately and came back with one of our pastors, who prayed and commanded his spirit to come back to him, but all to no avail. Wow!! It was too much to bear but after much tears and anguish, I had to accept the truth that was obvious and let go of my doubt and refusal to accept that fate.

Oh! What an emotionally draining time! Doubts, guilt, blame, and bitterness set in and took over my entire being. I blamed myself for not taking him to a better-equipped hospital; I blamed myself for allowing him to be transferred from the former hospital where he was before. All these thoughts were going across my mind, disturbing and getting me depressed. My situation now became worse than death. Even some people that came to 'comfort us' discouraged me, and the pain increased as they asked questions that were irrelevant to the situation. Others made remarks that made me feel infuriated.

And soon after this incident, my husband became very sick because he just came back from a trip, and met this horrible situation that threw him off balance. But thankfully, God began to give him strength, as healing came to his weak body, and my husband was completely made whole. However, sadly enough, the London suit that he bought for our son became his grave cloth. What a shame!

After a while, comfort began to come as the Holy Spirit ministered to us. He used some of the church leaders, who took it upon themselves to be visiting with us, and to pray with us too. The senior pastor and his wife became very close to us, as a source of consolation, having seen the depth of our ordeal. They employed the power of the Bible to help us see the promises of God to His people in times like these. They helped us to see that God was not to blame and that, sooner than expected, God would show Himself mighty in our family. And so, one by one, I began to forgive every one that offended me during that trying period.

To God be the glory, we trusted the word of God through his servant. In a short time, the Lord gave us another son, Joshua who is truly a child of consolation. I return all the glory to God, and give Him thanks to this day.

Pastor (Mrs.) Helen C. Njoku, Phd *is from Owerri , Imo State, Ngor Okpala L G A. She is the Proprietress of Covenant Group of Schools Elelenwo, Port Harcourt, R|S. She has the burning desire to reach out to young people to catch them young for God. It is also her heart desire to assist them to reach their academic height through hard work and self-confidence.*

With her training as a counselor, she is using her expertise to intensify efforts towards accelerating career development and guidance services to both students and parents. She is a member of Counseling Association of Nigeria [CASSON], Port Harcourt branch.

She is also a member of National Association of Proprietors of Private Schools [NAPPS], Port Harcourt chapter. Also, she is one of the facilitators of Professional Mentors Capacity Builders [PMCB], Port Harcourt branch. Helen is the coordinator of Widows Family Care Ministry [WFCM], Ngor Okpala, Port Harcourt chapters. To the glory of God, she is a pastor in Redemption Ministries, and the 1st vice president of Divine Daughters of Destiny International [DDDI].

By God's grace, she enjoys counseling children of all ages, including couples and widows.

Healed By Knowing

By Olu Sobanjo

bout 4 years ago, I was getting ready for VGC (our annual ladies' conference), which was to hold in Montreal, Canada. I lived in Kingston, Ontario at the time. Asides the conference, I was also getting ready to visit Nigeria with my boys—kids—for the very first time since I left the country and since they were born. As I was working out the logistics of the conference, I was working out the same for the trip. While all these were going on, I was also battling stomach ulcer. The symptoms were not new; Dr. Liz already prescribed a pill I could take as at when needed.

However, at a point in time, the same pill that worked like magic now became almost useless. Whenever I began to feel the pain, I would be very weak in my body, and would need time to recover even after I had eaten and taken the pills. It was a terrible episode like never before.

On the first day of the conference, I drove to Montreal (a 3-hours trip) and got there really sick. I almost didn't believe I could speak at the event but God helped me, as the pain subsided after much prayers and rest. The conference ended well; participants got a clearer understanding of the beauty that comes when one lives by faith and not by sight.

By the time I got back home to Kingston after the event, I was so tired but excited over such a wonderful weekend. I got all the stuffs I needed for the trip and packed the bags, and then we left for Nigeria the next day. The pain came intermittently till we boarded the plane. Before we left, I told my hubby that the pain was quite unbearable, and that I might need to fast and pray to battle the attacks. His response to me was about what God used to begin the process towards my healing—"Are you sure it's fasting that you need or faith?" At first, I felt uncomfortable with that comment. I replied, saying, "Are you trying to say that I don't believe God?"

As the Lord would have it, throughout my 3-week vacation in Nigeria, I didn't even remember the bags where I kept my tommy pills. I did not run to the pill, not even once throughout the trip—not until I got back to the hustle and bustle of the typical Canadian lifestyle. As soon as the pressures and the tasks began to increase, the pain began to return. That was when I began to wonder if this pain was stress related. I did a little study on the Internet and found out that many researches have classified ulcer as being highly stress and anxiety related.

Suddenly, I remembered what Ade said about believing in what God has done already. So I thought within me, my hubby may be right after all, the pain may be related to my faith level.

But then, I decided to begin a study. I began to question what was going on in my heart prior to each episode. God led me to write out all my worst fears and indeed, I had so much to write, and these included fear of people and fear of failure. Each day with God brought a new understanding of what Christ has done; and since it was clear that I was in need of a clear understanding, I began to stand on the word of God. Scriptures like:

Galatians 2:20 —

. . . .

I have been crucified with Christ. It is no longer I
who live, but Christ who lives in me. And the life
I now live in the flesh I live by faith in the Son of
God, who loved me and gave himself for me.

. . . .

Philippians 4:13 —

I can do all things through him who strengthens me.

Philippians 4:6 —

Do not be anxious about anything, but in everything by prayer and supplication with thanksgiving let your requests be made known to God.

Matthew 6:27 —

And which of you by being anxious can add a single hour to his span of life?

1 Peter 2:24 —

He himself bore our sins in his body on the tree, that we might die to sin and live to righteousness. By his wounds you have been healed.

God has opened my eyes clearly over the past four years. I now know that when Jesus went on the cross, he took my pain and diseases upon Himself. Ulcer was dealt with on the cross and so I don't have to deal with it anymore. I don't have to worry about what people think of me or if I won't succeed in my endeavours. Whenever a negative thought begins to rise in my heart, I quickly remind myself of what I have and who I am in Christ. Instead of allowing anxiety to build up inside me, I let the joy of the Lord build up and so pain does not come at all. I am so grateful to God that I am healed in Christ.

Besides healing, I have discovered that the work done on the cross is a repositioning work. Jesus brought me into a place of son-ship with the Father. Therefore, there is so much I get to enjoy if only I believe.

And You can too!

Choose Jesus!

By Cary-Lee Carter

At a very young age, I was introduced to Jesus. I accepted Christ at the age of about 6 or 7, and I was filled with God's Holy Spirit with the evidence of speaking in tongues. I had an immediate interest in the manifestation of the Holy Spirit and deeply wanted to hear God's voice daily. I believe God spoke directly to me often.

As a young child, I wanted to share this new thing with everyone. I attended United Pentecostal Church (UPC) in my young school years, attended kids' Bible camps, and went to youth retreats. In my early teens, I attended Christian camps, and continued to witness Christ to my peers. I also experienced first-hand immediate, physical healing, and witnessed physical miracles. I was made to be an evangelist, to share God's limitless love with everyone out there.

The problem I started to experience was that in all of this, I had no sense of my value, my parents' marriage was disintegrating, my sister was struggling financially in school, and slowly I was drawn into a vortex of confusion and had no ability to control anything going on around me. Towards the end of high school, I had full-blown eating disorders that progressively became unmanageable.

In my early 20's after university, I fulfilled my lifelong dream to travel the world. I started with India. Unfortunately, I did not have a strong understanding of the value of my life or the value of other people's lives. I got mixed up in a demoralizing, controlling world of international smuggling. Everything was a commodity, and cash was the god, as I had completely lost sight of Jesus.

My life was spared at least three times from death and imprisonment, and yet I could not see that God had protected me again and again.

This corrupt way of living lasted several years. The lifestyle I lived was hetaeristic and had no purpose except to make money and spend it. Every new opportunity to make more money I accepted, with no fear of the repercussions because I had no value on my life or those that I brought into this unscrupulous, treacherous lifestyle. Gold, guns, drugs, money laundering, and passport forgeries are just some of the double-dealing, profiteering ventures I yielded to.

After many failed attempts to leave, and extract myself from this way of life, I had only one place, one person to turn to, even Jesus.

I spent many nights on the balcony of my condo in Singapore crying out to God to save me, spiritually, emotionally, and physically. Little did I know that Jesus was about to save me.

Due to the severity of my anorexia, one late night, I found myself waking up to a bright light, with a voice saying, "Will you choose life?" (I was in the emergency department due to prolonged dehydration, and my kidneys were shutting down.) God was giving me a choice; even in the face of death, He can give us a choice, and I said to Him, "I choose life." When I finally laid down my life and completely yielded to Christ, God was victorious, and I was free.

During this time, I was also spontaneously healed of my 6 years of very painful anorexia, and was given a new lease on my life. The value and importance of why we exist, and why in our DNA we are designed to worship and love others, was supernaturally imparted to me.

I turned my life around and pursued the will of God in all areas of my life, pressing in, seeking the sweet spot of intimacy with Him, which I once had during my early youthful days. Because of the tender walk with Jesus in my youth, I always remembered and desired to be back in that sweet place, safe and protected, and hearing His voice.

In 1995, at about 11 years of living overseas, I moved with my two babies from Singapore to Colorado. I raised them with prayer and in my Christian faith. At that time, their Dad became very abusive and fraudulent about who he was and what he believed. I was devastated and felt very, very alone and scared. I sought help and counselling in my church, and I prayed relentlessly for healing or a release from this nightmare. I was eventually released from the situation and with God's plan and awesome provision, I returned to Canada with my two babies.

The next phase of my life had me completely reliant on the Lord. I purposed to read my Bible every day and meditate on His word and listen for direction and guidance daily. My spiritual muscles began to grow big and strong. God spoke directly to me in Colorado and told me exactly how, when and what He would do for us there. I had to trust Him completely.

I arrived in Canada safely with my two children and I had a house waiting for us. God continued in an omnipotent way to provide for us and fulfill all my heart's desires. He spoke clearly to me that I would get married within five years.

I pressed in at church and had to consult with my pastors, to find out what I must do to be prepared and ready, and be completely made whole. I sought out how to be the best that I could be, to be ready for this joyful day. I received healing from rejection, and God gave me the spirit of boldness. I went through several training courses and I had a personal mentor friend walk with me weekly for a year for my healing and development. During this season, a strong prophetic gifting with words of knowledge began to blossom in my life. In addition, the Lord showed me visions of me speaking and sharing the gospel, the Good News. He showed me how Jesus really loves people, and that nothing they have ever done or will do, will ever disqualify them of His love, purpose and destiny He has for each one.

I met and married my husband, Kurt Carter exactly five years after my arrival in Kingston as the Lord had promised I would. Kurt and I were sweethearts to each other in high school. Back then, I had many opportunities to witness to him. We were far too young and undeveloped then to make any commitment to each other.

Kurt became a Christian two years after our friendship ended in high school and he called me to let me know he was saved and would be baptized soon.

25 years later, we married!!!

Our life together has been AWESOME and very spiritually edifying. Together, we have been challenged, stretched, and forced to grow out of our comfort zones. Being together in the presence of God and His Holy Spirit is so tangible when we are in one accord as a couple fellowship with God. We speak the same language. We get the kingdom. Together, we desire to serve others, show the unconditional love of Christ, and regularly invite people into our home and family. We love to disciple and see healing and freedom grow in our new friends' lives. Together, we have seen several people got saved. We have seen lives radically transformed, both in North America and overseas (sometimes by telephone conversions). We desire to be barometers of integrity and righteousness in our personal lives and in the business community.

As we walk closely with the Lord, it is our desire to create a new thing for Him. We believe the Lord wants a new thing in Kingston; He is seeking a place of intimacy where the Lord finds our praises attractive. We believe the Lord wants to inhabit the praise in our church with a new song, which should be a place of spontaneous, unearthly, and anointed music. Our church should be a place of transparent intimacy, where all are loved, healed, and encouraged to grow and maximize their own promise in Jesus Christ. It is our desire to see all come to Christ, receive healing, and get their release into their full, glorious potential!

This is part of my story, and I share it to give you hope, to give you God's promise that He will never leave you, nor will He ever forsake you. You are valued, you are loved, and God has a mighty purpose and plan for your life if you will only chose Jesus.

Cary-Lee *is a dynamic, inspiring Leader, Speaker, Pastor, Church Planter, Teacher, Mother, Lifestyle Evangelist and a strong Prophetic voice to this generation.*

She is a passionate, intentional leader that encourages people to love others like Jesus did every day. For her it is a lifestyle not an infrequent activity. She is a hands-on leader that demonstrates by example. She believes strongly that you cannot lead people to a place that you have not gone yourself.

Cary-Lee is a global Christian with a perspective that is gleaned from having lived in, and travelled to, over 30 countries. Just like the Apostle Paul she has experienced both the highs and lows of having great abundance and learning to make do with very little. By the grace of God she escaped death and imprisonment multiple times and she has partici-

pated in many types of ministry. She has led many to Christ both personally and through her ministry. Her life's journey has shaped and moulded her into one who chooses life and freedom and she guides others into pursuing the presence, healing and love of the Father.

She is a magnetic advocate for the marginalized and the hurting as well as those who are rich in this world but not towards God. She unequivocally promotes the Word of God as our moral compass, not the morality of the day.

She and her husband Kurt Carter are the founding pastors of Church Without Borders, a growing congregation in Kingston, Ontario.

4

Other Facts

God Cares about His Own.

He cares about His own. No good gift will He with-hold from those who walk uprightly (Psalm 84: 11). If it feels like God has forgotten you, it's a lie that the enemy wants you to hold onto. You must be bold to tell him that's not true, first of all, because your uprightness is not from your good behaviours or your actions; but accepting Jesus into your life gave you the gift of righteousness. You became upright through Jesus. And because you are upright, God would not withhold anything good from Christ; He won't with-hold anything good from you; except peradventure He is trying to teach me something new about entrusting my life to Him.

God Doesn't Always Answer Us, As We Want.

Many of the prayers we say to God are not in tune with the plan that God has for us. Sometimes God would rather teach us a lesson than answer our prayers. As a Mom, I don't always answer my kids' request the way they want it. I answer those requests that will align with the plans I have for the family or for them.

This reminds me of an incidence that happened about 3 years go. I needed to pick up something from the Dollar Store with my kids. Knowing how tempting the experience would be for them, I decided that, this time, I would teach them a lesson. I brought out two Toonies ($2 coins) and gave one to each child. The plan was that each child could pick anything they wanted with the money as long as the money would be enough. So they were both excited. Of course, even adults know that is easier said than done. However, since I wanted to teach them a lesson, I was bent on following through this time. Both of them picked some simple toys (I can't remember may be cars or things like that), and I also picked up what I needed. However, as we turned to go to the cash register to pay for the items, my youngest son, who must have been three or so at the time, saw a bag of chips and said, "I want chips!"

Bags of chips were not usually on my grocery list at the time but when I did buy chips, it would be from the wholesale store. At this particular time, I knew we had a few huge bags of chips at home, so I told him, "You can have chips as soon as we get home in about five minutes times." Well, that was not what he wanted, he wanted the chip NOW! Moreover, that was when I found another moment, as a Mom, to drive home a lesson. I said to myself that I must stand my grounds here, to help this boy learn a quick lesson. At this time, he already had the bag of chips in his hands, and was wailing and decided to proceed with it to the cash register. I did not want to take it from him and put it back myself, I wanted him to learn by putting it back by himself. And of course, I didn't know what the reaction would be if I took it from him in the middle of the store. I didn't want to make a show.

Anyway, I moved along the aisle with both boys towards the counter, and they had what they wanted to buy with their Toonies. One of them had a bag of chip in his hands and wailed along the aisle, saying, "I want chips." Mind you, this experience wasn't easy for me; in my heart, I wasn't sure what the result of my teachable moments would be for that day. I wasn't sure if it was necessary, if it would teach him the lesson or if I would have to carry him out of the store that day. It was also a bit embarrassing because other shoppers could hear us, and many might have been thinking, "Common, it's just a bag of chip; buy it for the boy and give us some peace here."

I summoned courage despite all this thoughts, and continued to insist that he would get chips (the same kind) when we got home and that he should return the bag. I put all my merchandise on the cashier's table and paid for each item while my son continued to wail and scream. As I was completing my transaction, the cashier and shoppers on the queue were looking at me funny. And as soon as we were done with all payment, I said to my son one last time gently, "Go and return that to the shelf over there," and to my amazement, the same child had been wailing uncontrollably, stopped abruptly, ran back to the shelf, dropped off the bag of chips, and ran back to me. While I waited for him excitedly, he ran back like an hero, his big brother opened the door for us, and we matched majestically to the car and drove off. You can imagine how I felt like a hero myself. I was glad to leave a message in the mind of the other shoppers that, training a child may not be easy but it works. And of course, my son couldn't wait till we got home so he could get his chips. It was very interesting.

We May Never Know Why

You see, just the same way I had a plan set out for the family, the same way I seized a learning opportunity, and it's similar to the way God seizes one. There are many prayers I've prayed that God didn't answer, and so many cries seem to go on for too long. For some of them, I look back and thank Him for not answering my prayers the way I wanted it; and some others, I never got why He did not. I remember, on a certain day, I prayed that our electricity should be restored but He did not answer the prayer. In Nigeria, at this time, power supply was a problematic issue, and so the electric company would ration power to different neigbourhood, thus leaving each household responsible for generating their own power needs. One more thing is that getting fuel to run our generator was also another pain.

Since our inverter was not fully charged, we knew it would not sustain us for more than a few hours of the night. That mean we would have to sleep in the hot weather conditions, with no power to run our fans.

That was why we cried out to the Lord, so that power could be restored that night. During this time, I was writing this book, and I wanted to sit at my desk till the late hours of the night.

The truth is that we go through things at times and hope that God would hear our cry but He might not answer. So we feel bewildered. God is the all-knowing one—He knows what's best and to Him, it's about the big plan. It's not about my little family here. He won't go ahead and answer my prayers by all means and at the expense of other people and other plans that He has. So as you pray or cry to God, believe that He can do it and will do it, as long as it aligns with His original plans. Take time to study what His plans are. In some cases, like my prayers the other night I just referred to, it's not easy to know what His plans are.

How could we tell if His intent was to help us avert a disaster like electrocution or fire outbreak? We couldn't tell. That might be a reason why we forgot to buy fuel to supplement what we had in the generator, that day. We don't know all that. We prayed because we wanted our own comfort. In my mind, I didn't want the boys to suffer from heat rash. As for me, I wanted to have a sweet sleep, but God did not answer it that way.

The truth is that I may never understand why He didn't always answer my prayers, at least, the way I wanted it. It's important to be at peace within me, especially when it seems the answer is not forthcoming.

Stand On His Words Otherwise

Now, there are other times that you can see it clearly, as to what the Scriptures say about your situation. For example, God says there will be no one barren in our land, meaning that if you are a child of God, you will be fruitful in marriage. If you pray about it and you don't see the answer yet, you don't assume that it's not God's plans for you. You don't get mad that He doesn't care, and you don't unconsciously resign to such a fate that you may remain barren all your life. What you do is, trust that He will not withhold a child from you.

. . . .

Ps 84: 11 ESV — For the Lord God is a sun and shield; the Lord bestows favor and honor. No good thing does he withhold from those who walk uprightly.

. . . .

However, remember to rejoice if the answer is not yet there. As your faith in Him grows concerning the issue, you will begin to find joy to hold, because of the fact that He has promised it.

. . . .

Hebrews 11:6 — And without faith it is impossible to please him, for whoever would draw near to God must believe that he exists and that he rewards those who seek him.

. . . .

God honors our faith in Him. However, He sometimes chooses to arrange things differently than we plan them. He is always excited to demonstrate His power when we place our hope in Him.

Take Your Possession

At other times, He wants us to go against what is real to us in the physical. He wants us to challenge situations according to what the Word says. At times, the situation we are fighting against has its root-cause engrained in the history and bloodline of our lineage. Sometimes, we, or our loved ones, might make covenants on our behalf. Some fathers and mothers—ancestors of a lineage—make covenants with the devil to serve him, thereby bringing unborn generations into bondage. When you give your life to Christ, you need to cut off from any known or unknown covenants, especially those plaguing your life in any area.

The truth is that when Jesus died, He broke off the devil's right to punish us. He set us free. However, we must stand on that redemptive work of Christ, break the chains that tie us down, hide behind the cross that brought us freedom, and stand on that freedom.

. . . .

Ephesians 1: 18-22 NLT — *I pray that your hearts will be flooded with light so that you can understand the confident hope he has given to those he called—his holy people who are his rich and glorious inheritance. I also pray that you will* understand the incredible greatness of God's power for us who believe him. This is the same mighty power that raised Christ from the dead and seated him in the place of honor at God's right hand in the heavenly realms. Now he is far above any ruler or authority or power or leader or anything else—not only in this world but also in the world to come. God has put all things under the authority of Christ and has made him head over all things for the benefit of the church.

· ·

Break away from covenants that have been established for your benefit; break free from the ones with whom you have entered into covenants. You can denounce them, and hide behind Christ, who has given you victory through His shed blood.

· ·

Isaiah 49:24-25 — Can the prey be taken from the mighty, or the captives of a tyrant be rescued? For thus says the LORD: 'Even the captives of the mighty shall be taken, and the prey of the tyrant be rescued, for I will contend with those who contend with you, and I will save your children.'

· ·

As Kids

At times, we claim to agree with the word of God but we really don't. It's just like when kids easily agree that something belongs to them. Take a kid to a public park and he can easily take possession of a toy when no other kids are there. However the story may change when stronger kids arrive. When you begin to stand on the word of God, it may start as a weak grip, don't stop there—don't let anyone or anything distract you. Continue to hold onto the Word until you are so sure that nothing can make you doubt that God is alive, and is with you ALWAYS!

5

Treasure Chest

This book was intended to give you a boost in your faith, and I am sure your hope in Christ is being built. In order to help you further, I want you to look at the following Scriptures as a tool sharpen you, and enhance your faith, based on the theme of this book. It's your turn now to study God's word concerning your current situation.

Let me reiterate that the aim of this book is to help you to understand fully that God has not forgotten you. The reason you may feel stranded in life is that you are going through a storm of life. As you look through God's words, you will see that there is a solution for every single situation. Our God is stronger than any storm. He did calm the storm by commanding peace to come. You can do the same; remember He is still alive in you.

Pray the following prayer first and then take time to read the Scriptures below, and note everything that comes to your heart after reading each scripture, especially the ones that affect your situation the most. Then write out your thoughts at the end of each scripture reading.

Pray this:

Dear Lord, open my eyes to see the wonderful truths in you instructions (Psalm 119:18). Please, give me spiritual wisdom and insight so that I may grow in the knowledge of you, Lord. And please, flood my heart with light so that I can understand the confident hope that you have given to me in Christ. Please, help me to understand the incredible greatness of your mighty power (Ephesians 1:17-19). Help me to know that I can do greater things as you did because I am in you and you are in me. In Jesus' name, I pray. Amen! (John 14:12)

Hebrews 11:1 *Now faith is the assurance (title deed, confirmation) of things hoped for (divinely guaranteed), and the evidence of things not seen [the conviction of their reality—faith comprehends as fact what cannot be experienced by the physical senses]. (AMP)*

_____

_____

_____

_____

Hebrews 11:6 *But without faith it is impossible to please Him, for he who comes to God must believe that He is, and that He is a rewarder of those who diligently seek Him (NKJV)*

_____

_____

_____

_____

Ps 84: 11 ESV — *For the Lord God is a sun and shield; the Lord bestows favor and honor. No good thing does he withhold from those who walk uprightly.*

_____

_____

_____

_____

Psalm 89:34 — *I will not violate my covenant or alter the word that went forth from my lips.*

_____

_____

_____

_____

1 John 2:25 — *This is the promise, which He Himself made to us: eternal life.*

_____

_____

_____

_____

Luke 18:27 — *But he said, What is impossible with man is possible with God.*

_____

_____

_____

_____

Ezekiel 36:26 — *Moreover, I will give you a new heart and put a new spirit within you; and I will remove the heart of stone from your flesh and give you a heart of flesh.*

_____

_____

_____

_____

1 John 1:9 — *If we confess our sins, He is faithful and righteous to forgive us our sins and to cleanse us from all unrighteousness.*

_____

_____

_____

_____

Psalm 103:12 — *As far as the east is from the west, So far has He removed our transgressions from us.*

_____

_____

_____

_____

Micah 7:19 — *He will again have compassion on us; He will tread our iniquities under foot Yes, You will cast all their sins into the depths of the sea.*

_____

_____

_____

_____

Galatians 5:22-23 — *But the fruit of the Spirit is love, joy, peace, patience, kindness, goodness, faithfulness, gentleness, self-control; against such things there is no law.*

_____

_____

_____

_____

Psalm 34:4 — *I sought the LORD, and He answered me, And delivered me from all my fears.*

_____

_____

_____

_____

Isaiah 49:25 — *Surely, thus says the LORD, "Even the captives of the mighty man will be taken away, And the prey of the tyrant will be rescued; For I will contend with the one who contends with you, And I will save your sons.*

_____

_____

_____

_____

Luke 11:13 — *If you then, being evil, know how to give good gifts to your children, how much more will your heavenly Father give the Holy Spirit to those who ask Him?*

_____

_____

_____

_____

Philippians 4:19 — *And my God will supply all your needs according to His riches in glory in Christ Jesus.*

_____

_____

_____

_____

Romans 8:32 — *He who did not spare His own Son, but delivered Him over for us all, how will He not also with Him freely give us all things?*

_____

_____

_____

_____

James 1:5 — *But if any of you lacks wisdom, let him ask of God, who gives to all generously and without reproach, and it will be given to him.*

Isaiah 26:3 — *The steadfast of mind You will keep in perfect peace, Because he trusts in You.*

---

1 Corinthians 10:13 — *No temptation has overtaken you but such as is common to man; and God is faithful, who will not allow you to be tempted beyond what you are able, but with the temptation will provide the way of escape also, so that you will be able to endure it.*

Jeremiah 30:17 — *For I will restore you to health And I will heal you of your wounds, declares the LORD, 'Because they have called you an outcast, saying: 'It is Zion; no one cares for her.'*

_____

_____

_____

Psalm 91:4-6 — *He will cover you with His pinions, And under His wings you may seek refuge; His faithfulness is a shield and bulwark. You will not be afraid of the terror by night, Or of the arrow that flies by day; Of the pestilence that stalks in darkness, Or of the destruction that lays waste at noon.*

_____

_____

_____

_____

John 5:28-29 — *Do not marvel at this; for an hour is coming, in which all who are in the tombs will hear His voice, and will come forth; those who did the good deeds to a resurrection of life, those who committed the evil deeds to a resurrection of judgment.*

_____

_____

_____

_____

John 14:2-3 — *In My Father's house are many dwelling places; if it were not so, I would have told you; for I go to prepare a place for you. "If I go and prepare a place for you, I will come again and receive you to Myself, that where I am, there you may be also.*

_____

_____

_____

_____

Revelation 21:4 — *and He will wipe away every tear from their eyes; and there will no longer be any death; there will no longer be any mourning, or crying, or pain; the first things have passed away.*

_____

_____

_____

_____

6

Your Testimony

All right! You have made it to the end of this book. What a great thing to know who and where you are in Christ! This is your section of the book. You will take a moment to recount a particular thing that God has done in your life in the past. Remember the details and use the space below to write it out. After this exercise, I will recommend that you prayerfully find another person in need of hope around you and share the book with them or tell them your story, to encourage them to put their hope in God. In this process, you don't need to try to change their mindset, simply trust the Holy Spirit to use your story to touch their heart.

Here is a good format to follow:

Before you start...

Firstly, pray that God will reveal Himself to the person you will share the book or your story with. Pray in the Spirit, if you can, for as long as you have the time to or feel led to.

Secondly, read Acts 26 (It's an account of Paul telling his testimony).

Focus on the 3-step structure below. I call it Recommended Testimony Structure.

The Before: What was the key problem, emotion, situation, or attitude you were dealing with?

The Catalyst: The solution — Identify how God helped bring the solution. Take time to show steps that brought you to the point of trusting in Christ.

The After: How have your thoughts, attitudes, emotions, and relationships changed since then?

Here You Go!

_____

_____

_____

_____

_____

_____

_____

_____

_____

_____

_____

_____

_____

_____

_____

_____

_____

_____

_____

_____

_____

_____

_____

_____

_____

_____
_____
_____
_____
_____
_____
_____
_____
_____
_____
_____
_____
_____
_____
_____
_____
_____
_____
_____
_____
_____
_____
_____

_____
_____
_____
_____
_____
_____
_____
_____
_____
_____
_____
_____
_____
_____
_____
_____
_____
_____
_____
_____
_____
_____

About the Authors

Olu (Oluwaseun) Sobanjo is passionate about Christ. Working alongside her husband, Ade, she serves as co-pastor at Overcomers Assembly since its inception in 2005. After planting three branches in different locations in Canada, Olu and her family moved to Nigeria, where they are currently serving the Lord, at a mission church they planted in a community called Kuje, near Abuja, Nigeria; the Churches continue to be home for ordinary people living extraordinary lives.

She is mother to two wonderful boys (Demi & Damilola). Olu is a mentor and inspiration to women everywhere. She loves to help and see people pursue a thriving life in Christ.

Her desire to meet the needs of women led her to start the women's ministry (single and married) at her church. She hosts the Vessels of Grace Conference (an annual women's conference), which kicked off in May 2007.

She had a fulfilling career in financial planning for about 5 years until she left the practice in July 2012 to devote herself to full-time ministry. She enjoys pursuing Christ daily.

Rev Mrs Regina M. Kehinde is the senior Pastor of Day-Spring Foursquare Fellowship Church, Queens, New York.

She is married with children and grandchildren. She preaches and teaches the Word without fear or favor. She is a Christian Educator per excellence. As a dynamic Sunday school curriculum designer and developer, she is ready to help any church or group to put their Sunday school and teaching ministry in the right perspective with results.

Other Books by Olu Sobanjo

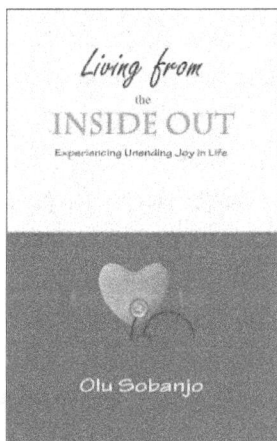

In today's fast paced world, you can assume that doing certain spiritual activity regularly is what brings joy in Christ.

In this insightful book, Olu challenges readers to constantly look within in order to experience Christ's abundant life. She provides biblical insights and draws from her personal experience to illustrate how life in Christ can become richer and stronger.

Olu says; if you would make surrendering a part of your daily life you will start experiencing the unending joy of knowing Christ: thriving in life like Jesus; from the inside out.

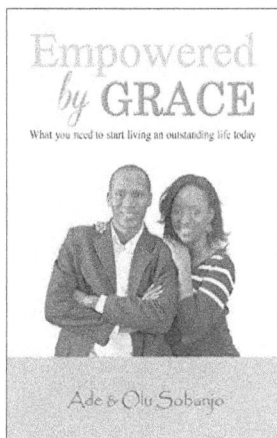

It's high time the world sees the manifestations of the sons and daughters of God.

If you are ready to enter fully into your purpose in life through Christ, then you need to read this book.

Ade and Olu Sobanjo explain what you need to know and do to enjoy God grace that is available for you already. You can begin your work today.

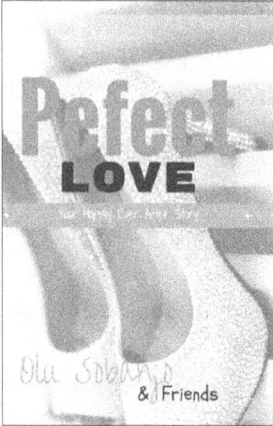

Do happily ever afters only happen in fairy tales?

No! You can have your personal story transformed in the arms of a loving Father, who loves you so perfectly and will do anything to get you into this wonderful story of love.

Olu Sobanjo and her friends have compiled a rich package for you in the book Perfect Love; Your happily ever after story.

Get ready to be blown away by the love of your precious King.

All titles Available on Amazon or wherever books are sold.

www.ingramcontent.com/pod-product-compliance
Lightning Source LLC
Chambersburg PA
CBHW021127020426
42331CB00005B/649